KING Josiah and GOD'S Book

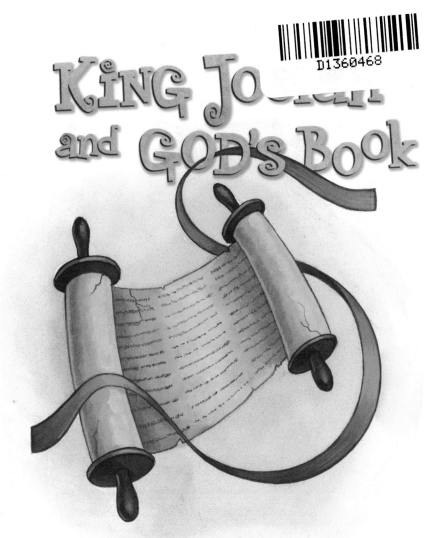

Josiah renews the covenant

2 Kings 22:1–23:27 for children

Written by Kristin R. Nelson
Illustrated by Shawna J. C. Tenney

CONCORDIA PUBLISHING HOUSE · SAINT LOUIS

Josiah was only eight years old
When he became a king.
He soon learned to love the Lord
And followed God in everything.

But his people who lived in Judah
Were naughtier than most.
And poor Josiah couldn't help much;
He had no rules to post.

Till one day he saw the temple
Had fallen in disrepair.
"We have got to fix this place,"
King Josiah did declare.

And during all the cleaning,
A special book was found—
The Book of Law—inside which
God's rules for life were bound.

The high priest of the temple
Was the first to find the book.
He passed it to a secretary
Who also took a look.

The secretary ran to the king
Who read the book straight through.
Then King Josiah tore his robes
For the sins that he now knew.

"There're going to be some changes here,"
Said Josiah with disgust.
"Our faith must lie in our true God.
In Him we place our trust."

So Josiah sent an invitation
To all the people in his land:
To the poor, the meek, the shabby,
To the rich, the strong, the grand.

When they had all gathered,
Josiah began to read
All the words of God's to follow
In thought and word and deed.

After Josiah finished reading
The book of God's commands,
He said, "I promise to try to keep
All the Lord's demands."

Then he asked the sinful people
To turn their hearts to God.
"Yes, we'll follow this Book of Law,"
Josiah's people said with a nod.

Then the changes started coming
Like Josiah said they would.
And God smiled upon Josiah
Whose heart was pure and good.

First, false idols were rounded up
And burned outside the city gate.
Then Josiah destroyed everything
He thought that God would hate.

Josiah didn't forget the people
Who led the wicked ways.
He permanently removed their evil
From Judah's nights and days.

But our good King Josiah
Didn't just say, "No! No!"
He knew a special celebration
Would help his people's faith to grow.

"I propose that every year
A Passover feast be planned.
We must remember how our great God
Delivered us from Egypt's land."

Not for hundreds of years had anyone
Celebrated Passover night.
But now the people showed their love
For God was pure and right.

No other king had turned to God so fully
With all his strength and soul and heart.
His faithfulness never wavered;
Nor did his love for God depart.

Dear Parents,

The Bible had been put away and forgotten. The Israelites had again turned from God. And again, God sent them a leader—King Josiah—to bring them back to Him.

Josiah was a conscientious king who was proud of his land. In his efforts to preserve his national heritage, the Book of the Law—a portion of the Scriptures that contained the Commandments—was rediscovered. Josiah's first reaction was to recognize his own shortcomings and then turn from his sinful ways. King Josiah then invited his people to do the same. He renewed his nation's commitment to the covenant. Throughout his land and even into other nations, Josiah led the way to the destruction of false idols and wicked practices (such as fortune-telling, prostitution, and even child sacrifice). For a world that had worshiped idols for centuries, this move was a dramatic cultural shift. Josiah also reinstituted the Passover observance. This act was as significant as the others. God commanded the Passover feast. Indeed, it was the Passover lamb that foreshadowed the Lamb of God. By reinstituting the Passover, Josiah helped the children of Israel hear the Gospel.

Like John the Baptist, King Josiah called the people to repentance and to prepare for the Lamb of God. Our pastors do the same when they preach the Gospel and administer the Sacraments in today's churches. Like King Josiah, our pastors remind us of God's Law, the mirror that shows us our sin and our need for the Lamb: our Savior who takes away our sin.

The message of this Bible story for your child is that our patient, loving God sends His servants to remind us of His mercy and teach us His Word. He gives us direction for our lives. And when we sin, He provides us with forgiveness through the blood of His Son, Jesus Christ.

The Editor